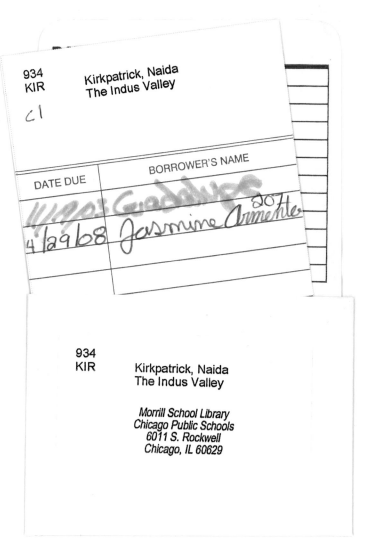

934
KIR   Kirkpatrick, Naida
         The Indus Valley

c1

DATE DUE	BORROWER'S NAME
4/29/68	Jasmine Armente

The Indus Valley

NAIDA KIRKPATRICK

Heinemann Library
Chicago, Illinois

C 1   2003   19.95

Design and map illustrations by Depke Design
Illustrations on pages 12 and 57 by J. Mark Kenoyer
Illustrations on pages 14T, 14B and 61 by Heinemann Library
Printed and bound in the United States by Lake Book Manufacturing, Inc.

06 05 04 03 02
10 9 8 7 6 5 4 3 2 1

Library of Congress Cataloging-in-Publication Data
Kirkpatrick, Naida.
  The Indus Valley / Naida Kirkpatrick.
     p. cm. -- (Understanding people in the past)
Includes bibliographical references and index.
Summary: Provides an introduction to the Harappa people who lived in the
Indus Valley thousands of years ago, describing their civilization,
daily life, religious beliefs, and more.
  ISBN: 1-58810-424-9 (HC), 1-4034-0099-7 (Pbk.)
  1. Indus civilization--Juvenile literature. [1. Indus civilization.]
I. Title. II. Series.
  DS425 .K54 2002
  934--dc21
                        2001005326

Acknowledgments
The author and publisher are grateful to the following for permission to reproduce copyright material:

Cover photograph courtesy of © J. Mark Kenoyer

Title page, pp. 5T, 8, 9, 10, 11T, 13T, 13B, 15T, 15B, 18T, 18B, 19, 20, 21, 22B, 23B, 25, 26, 27T, 27B, 28, 29, 32, 33, 34, 36T,
37, 39, 40T, 40B, 41, 43, 44T, 44B, 45, 46, 48, 50, 54, 55, 59B H. A. R. P. and Courtesy of the Department of Archaeology
and Museums, Pakistan; pp. 4T, 6, 7, 30, 35T, 38, 42, 49, 51, 53, 58, 59T © J. Mark Kenoyer; p. 11B Jehangir
Gazdar/Woodfin Camp & Associates; pp. 16, 47 Christopher Klein/NGS Image Collection; p. 17 © J. Mark Kenoyer,
courtesy Chris Sloan, artist; pp. 22T, 23T, 31 Jehangir Gazdar/Woodfin Camp & Associates, courtesy of the Department
of Archaeology and Museums, Pakistan; pp. 24, 35T Randy Olson/NGS Image Collection; p. 36B Dilip Mehta/Woodfin
Camp & Associates; pp. 52, 57 NGSMAPS/NGS Image Service.

Special thanks to J. Mark Kenoyer for his comments in the preparation of this book and
also for providing many of the images found in this book.

Every effort has been made to contact copyright holders of any material reproduced in this book.
Any omissions will be rectified in subsequent printings if notice is given to the publisher.

Some words are shown in bold, **like this.** You can find out what they
mean by looking in the glossary.

A note about dates: in this book, dates are followed by the letters B.C.E.
(Before the Common Era) or C.E. (Common Era). This is used instead of
the older abbreviations B.C. and A.D. The date numbers are the same in
both systems.

Contents

Who Lived in the Indus Valley?

From 2600 until 1300 B.C.E. the Harappan people lived and worked in the region known as the Indus Valley. The greater Indus Valley is the land along the banks of the Indus and Ghaggar-Hakra Rivers. It covers parts of the countries we know now as Pakistan and India.

The land along the sides of the river is good for growing crops. Away from the river, the land is a desert of sand and rocky mountains.

The Himalaya mountains provide a source of water to the Indus River. The mountains also provide good hunting, timber, minerals, and semi-precious stones.

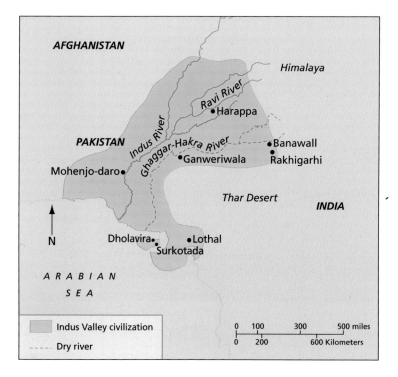

This map shows the ancient Indus Valley civilization. Most of the area was near water.

4

The people who lived in the ancient Indus Valley are called Harappans. No one knows exactly what the Harappan people looked like. They were farmers and **merchants.** They hunted and fished. Their system of **trade** extended throughout the region.

We know the Harappans were creative. Many **figurines,** pieces of pottery, and pieces of metalwork have been found in the Indus Valley. They also made beautiful jewelry.

The Harappans made many different types of pottery.

The Harappans

No one actually knows the real name of the ancient Indus city known as Harappa. The name was borrowed from the modern town built on top of the ancient mounds. The people of the Indus Valley soon became known by others as Harappans.

Gift of the Indus River

Summer in the Indus Valley is hot—the temperature reaches more than 100°F (38°C). In the winter, the temperature can fall below 0°F (-32°C). There are six seasons: spring, summer, rainy, autumn, winter, and dewy.

Along the river

The Harappans built cities and settlements along the Indus River. When the rivers flooded, it naturally watered their crops. They also relied on rainwater during the winter season. They established **trade** routes along the river.

The Indus River provided for many of the ancient Harappans' needs.

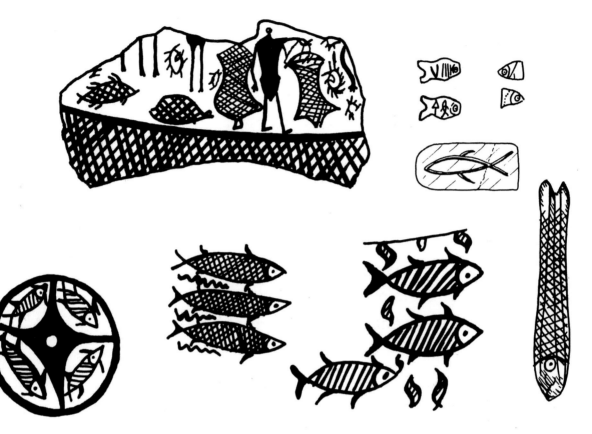

Fishing

Fishing methods have not changed much along the Indus River. The Harappans used a hook and line, as well as nets, to catch carp, catfish, eels, and blind porpoises from the river. They also caught turtles, snails, and clams. The people living along the coast of the Arabian Sea had different kinds of fish and shellfish. Fish could be preserved by drying, so they could be eaten later.

The Harappans liked to eat fish and shellfish. We know this because pictures of fish have been found on much of their pottery and **inscribed tablets.**

How Do We Know About the Harappans?

In 1850, British engineers began to build a railroad in the **Punjab,** an area in northern India. They collected and crushed brick that was scattered on ancient mounds to use beneath the railroad tracks. These mounds were really ancient cities along a **trade** route. **Archaeologists** discovered that some mounds held important remains of the oldest cities in the region.

In 1920 the archaeologists continued **excavating** the mounds. They discovered the remains of a civilization of people who made beautiful objects from copper, bronze, and stone. These people had also made pottery, jewelry, and carved **figurines.** Their cities showed good engineering and planning. Some of their wells and buildings are still standing.

Ancient mounds

The Harappans were continually building houses and streets over earlier constructions. The walls around Harappa have been rebuilt at least three times. As a result of their rebuilding, the city gradually became a series of mounds. These mounds are what archaeologists saw in 1850.

This well is in the ancient city of Mohenjo-daro. It is made of brick, as were almost all of the buildings.

In 1920, Sir John Marshall and other archaeologists excavated two of the major cities—Mohenjo-daro in the south and Harappa in the north. They knew these were major cities because they were very large. Other explorations have discovered additional cities, but these two are the most explored and well known.

Archaeologists uncover the story of how ancient people lived and worked by studying **artifacts.** Usually, they have only fragments to examine.

Here, Pakistani and American archaeologists clear a circular brick platform. They carefully brush away the dust to uncover what is beneath.

After studying the remains of buildings and pieces of pottery, **archaeologists** determined that the Harappan cities were built between 2600 and 1300 B.C.E. The Harappan people did not leave behind monuments or large temples. Only smaller **artifacts** remain of their **culture.** Many **figurines** have been found, most only a few inches tall.

Seals

There are many **seals** with engraved figures showing animals and trees. One figure that appears very often is the unicorn. People may have believed that the unicorn protected and

Square stamp seals were used to identify a specific person or family. The image is facing left so that when the seal is pressed onto a clay **tablet,** the image will face the right. This unicorn seal is dated between 2450-2200 B.C.E.

guided them. The wild fig or "pipal" tree is also a common motif. This tree is thought to be a symbol of protection and the dwelling place of a **deity.** Other animals shown are **zebu,** water buffalo, goats, and even elephants.

Harappan writing

It is thought that cups and pottery were **inscribed** in order to show ownership. Some seals were made so a string could be attached and the seal worn about the neck or at the waist.

No one has been able to **decipher** the Harappan **script** yet. This is why it is difficult for archaeologists to figure out the names of Harappan cities, people, and animals. Once Harappan writing is deciphered, we will be able to learn a lot more about the culture.

This is a bronze figurine of a woman. She is holding an **offering** in a bowl, held in her right hand.

Harappan writing is still a mystery to scholars because there are no links to later writing systems.

From about 7000 to 3000 B.C.E., the people living in the Indus Valley region were living in small farming villages or towns. They grew wheat, barley, and other crops. They also raised sheep, goats, and cattle. Chipped stone was used for some tools and copper and bronze for others.

Houses

Their houses were small, rectangular, and made of mud-brick with wooden roofs covered in grass. Some houses had smaller storage rooms beneath the floor. People

This small house dates from 6500 B.C.E. **Archaeologists** believe that it is a typical house for the time.

would store grain and other valuable goods in these compartments.

Pottery

By comparing and contrasting the painted designs on pottery from this time, archaeologists have been able to conclude that there were distinct communities of people living in different areas.

The Indus civilization emerges

By about 2800 B.C.E., more and more large settlements became established in the Indus Valley itself. The once distinct groups of people began to live together in a more complex, organized society.

This pottery stand was made during the early part of the Harappan civilization. It shows that even then they had sophisticated pottery making skills.

Pottery made around 3000 B.C.E. was usually decorated. This pot has bird and net designs painted on it.

There have been many attempts by scholars to relate Indus **script** to that of other **cultures,** such as Mesopotamia and ancient Egypt. However, each of these writing systems is unique and reflects the needs of each culture. The people of the Indus Valley generally wrote from right to left. They had a script of about 400–450 signs. One symbol could mean several things.

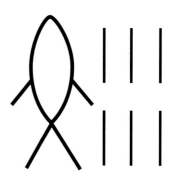

This figure possibly means "fish". It also could mean "shine," "glitter," or "flash" (like a star). Combine the symbol with six straight lines, and it could mean "six stars" or the constellation Plaeides.

An unknown language

Since no one has been able to **decipher** the Harappan language, we can only guess at the real meanings of the symbols. Harappan writing is not like any known script in ancient history. **Archaeologists** believe that the symbol on the far left means "basket" and that the symbol in the middle means "man." Together, the two symbols combine to possibly mean "basket carrier." Is this the symbol Harappans used when they wanted to describe someone who held baskets? No one knows—yet!

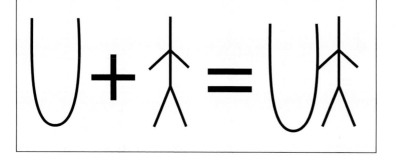

Ivory "counters" have been found in many different shapes. Ivory comes from elephant tusks. The Harappans might have hunted elephants themselves or **traded** with others for ivory.

Artifacts found by archaeologists show that the Harappans wrote by carving, cutting, or painting on pottery, terra-cotta, shell, bone, metal, or stone. One thing we know for certain is that they used writing to record numbers. Marks on pottery and **seals** appear to be indications of accounting.

The script on Harappan seals and pottery is usually no more than five or six symbols long.

We do not know who ruled the ancient cities of the Harappan civilization. Some cities may have been controlled by powerful leaders—kings or queens. Other cities may have been ruled by groups of individuals such as **merchants** and landowners.

Government officials

The leaders governed by controlling **trade** and collecting taxes. City officials were responsible for building and taking care

The Harappans loved processions, and many are shown on their **tablets.** A procession like the one in this illustration gave importance to the leaders of the city.

of the streets, houses, walls, and drains. They also were in charge of building the gateways and large buildings that were used by everyone for public meetings or fairs.

A city with good leaders became more powerful through trade and profit. Gateways and large public buildings showed the power of Indus Valley rulers. The major cities were far apart and each city had its own set of rulers.

This gateway has a room to the side of the entry. A gatekeeper was there to weigh goods being brought into the city and to collect taxes.

Women's clothes

Most **figurines** of women show them wearing short skirts, though they also sometimes wore long skirts. Many of the figurines of women show the hair pulled away from the face. Some of the figures of women appear to be wearing a **turban.**

Men's clothes

Stone sculptures of men show them wearing a long cloak over the left shoulder, leaving the right arm bare. A piece of cloth was worn around the waist, drawn through the legs, and tucked into the waistband at the back. Some of the men also wore fancy hairstyles.

This Harappan woman is wearing a necklace with beads and pendants. The belt around her skirt was also made of beads and copper.

This sculpture of the "Priest King" is from Mohenjo-daro. The cloak covers the left shoulder and has designs that indicate patterns of ancient Harappan cloth.

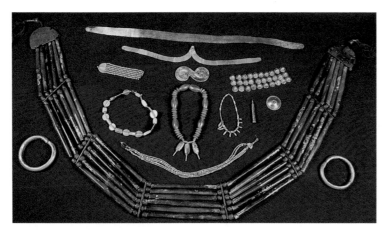

The Harappans made many types of jewelry. Here, there are bracelets, bangles, necklaces, and belts, made mostly from stone beads and gold.

Children's clothes

There are few figurines that have been found of children. **Archaeologists** believe that they dressed the same as adults.

Jewelry

We know the Harappans liked to wear jewelry. Many figurines show necklaces, belts, and head ornaments. Men and women both wore bracelets or **bangles.** Women and girls also wore many necklaces and belts. Men and boys wore necklaces with many beads and pendants close to their throats.

Necklaces of **carnelian** beads, shell, **lapis lazuli, turquoise,** agate, **faience,** and gold have been found by archaeologists. Bangles and necklaces of shell were found far from the coast. This shows that these items were **traded** all throughout the Indus Valley region.

Neighborhoods

Families lived in neighborhoods with people who did the same kind of work. Narrow streets divided each neighborhood. The homes of potters and metalworkers were often close to the edge of the city or outside the city wall. This was done so that the fumes and smoke of metalworking, along with the noise associated with other crafts, would not bother others. Some farmers lived in the city and went outside the wall during the day to work on their farms. People moved freely between neighborhoods.

Harappans lived in neighborhoods within the city walls. At Mohenjo-daro, closely packed houses from ancient times can still be seen.

Infant figurines like these were possibly meant to act as a prayer of protection and good health for a child.

Women

A woman's position in Harappan society was important. Powerful female **deities** have been found on **seals** alongside male deities. Some women may have become important **traders,** leaders, or priestesses.

Boys and girls

When a baby was born, there was much happiness. Many **figurines** of infants and children are male. In most areas, a boy probably learned the occupation of his father. If a man did not have a son to carry on his work, he may have taken an **apprentice.** Some figurines show women taking care of infants or grinding grain. These may have been toys for girls to teach them how to manage a household.

Growing Up and Going to School

The children of Harappa and Mohenjo-daro did not have schools like we have today, but they did have things to learn. Boys were taught the skills and work their fathers did.

Young girls were taught by their mothers how to cook, weave cloth, and take care of the family. Miniature household items such as beds and cooking pots have been found. Girls used these to help them learn how to run a household.

These miniature pots would have been used by Harappan girls learning to keep house.

Many toys and games have been found at Mohenjo-daro. Among these **artifacts** are stone balls, marbles, and clay dice.

This pottery toy ram with wheels was found at Mohenjo-daro.

Children's games

Archaeologists have found terra-cotta tops, clay marbles, and whistles. Children also had animal-shaped toys made with wheels so they would move. They learned about religion and social ideas by watching puppet theater and playing games. Many of the games are still being played today.

Pittu

Archaeologists in the Indus Valley have found clay disks in groups of three to seven. These disks vary in size and resemble a game called pittu that is still being played in the region today. The disks are stacked in the center of a circle of players. One player throws a ball to knock down the stack. Another player then re-stacks the disks while the others scatter in a game of tag. This game is close to 4,500 years old.

What Did the Harappans Believe?

The Harappan people were religious, but **archaeologists** have not found any special buildings or temples. Harappans may have made temporary worship areas out of bamboo or wood. They also appear to have worshipped beneath sacred trees, such as the pipal tree.

The pipal tree

The pipal tree has heart-shaped leaves. Harappans believed a god with horns lived in the pipal tree. Important religious ceremonies took place at the tree. The image of the pipal tree appears on many **seals** and pieces of pottery. One scene shows people holding water jars and bowing before the tree.

Archaeologists think that many important Harappan ceremonies took place near the pipal tree since it appears on so many **tablets** and seals.

This seal impression is from Harappa. It shows a **deity** standing under an arch of pipal leaves.

Marriage ceremonies might have taken place at the pipal tree. The pipal tree is believed to be a symbol of **fertility** and protection by Hindus today. This belief may have come from the Harappans.

Sacred symbols

The presence of sacred symbols on seals and pottery shows how important religious beliefs were to the Harappans' everyday lives. They have created many pictures and seals showing a unicorn. Unicorns were an important symbol to the Harappans.

Festivals and Rituals

Festivals and trade fairs

Religious festivals may have been held at the same time as **trade** fairs one or two times a year. **Merchants** would sell their goods and traveling artists would entertain people with puppet shows. Storytellers told legends and myths.

Water

Water was very important to the Harappans. They took extra care to build wells that would provide clean water. They also built drains that would carry dirty water and sewage away from houses.

The Harappans built many bathing platforms in their cities. The Great Bath at Mohenjo-daro was more than just a place to get clean. There was probably also a ceremony performed there using water.

Burials

Some Harappan burials contained a few bracelets and ornaments, but it seems they did not want to bury all their wealth. Special burial pots probably held water and food for the dead. The dead would need these things in the afterlife.

Painted pottery like this may have been used in Harappan ceremonies involving water.

Seals and figurines

There are **seals** showing figures kneeling before a **deity.** They also show special head ornaments and wreaths of pipal leaves.

Children were probably taught religion using masks and puppets made of clay or wood. People may have thought the unicorn would protect them in the real world as well as in the spirit world.

Many animal **figurines** suggest that animals may have been used as **sacrifices** in rituals. In some cases, figures made of terra-cotta or flour were used instead of real animals. Rituals required special tools or objects. One such object is a ritual **offering** stand. Special ladles made from shell were used for offerings of milk, oil, or butter.

Ritual offering stands were shown on seals and also carried in processions.

This **tablet** shows a man killing a water buffalo in the presence of a seated deity.

27

We do not know how Harappans treated injuries such as broken bones. Broken bones were probably "treated" by annoiting the limb with herbal medicines and wrapping it in cotton bandages. They might have tried to set the break. Severe injuries most likely became infected and the person died.

Barbers

Archaeologists have found instruments such as bronze razors, pins, and pincers. In modern south Asia, these tools are used by both a barber and a doctor. Many times a barber

Cups and ladles were made from shell. This cup could have been used for making **offerings** to the gods or for giving medicine.

The Harappans used copper to make blades like this. This blade could have been used for medicinal or other practical purposes.

and a doctor were the same person. As a barber, a man would cut hair and trim beards. As a doctor, he would chant to promote healing, cut the sick person to release bad spirits or fever, and prescribe herbal medicines for the illness.

Ritual specialists

Ritual specialists may have used herbs and special **incantations** to heal the sick. A bronze **figurine** of a woman holding a small bowl has been found. The bowl may have held an offering of food or oil to a **deity.** It is possible that ritual specialists believed an offering would help cure a sick person.

The Farming Year

Fall

In the fall, Harappans planted wheat and barley. Lentils, **sesamum,** vegetables, and possibly cotton were also planted. These crops were watered by the winter rains.

Summer

In the summer, they planted cotton, mustard, sesamum, dates, melon, and peas. These crops were harvested in the fall, if there was enough rainfall.

Irrigation canals were used in the highlands. Channels to divert water were dug and dams were built. In some of the small settlements, wells may have been used for watering gardens in the city.

Animals

Farmers used hoes or digging sticks as well as plows to **cultivate** the soil. The **zebu** is shown on many **seals** and would have been good for pulling carts and plows. Zebu are strong and well adapted to the heat.

The water buffalo was another work animal. Farmers made butter from the milk of the water buffalo.

These terraced fields are similar to the fields used by Indus farmers. Terraced fields are built into the side of a hill like a series of flat steps. This makes it easier to raise crops in hilly areas.

Goats and sheep were kept for meat and dairy products, as well as wool. Many terra-cotta **figurines** of peacocks, pheasants, pigeons, and ducks have been uncovered. Other wild animals shown on pottery and seals are antelope, gazelles, deer, wild pigs, and rhinoceroses.

Tigers and leopards were a threat to Harappan farmers. They would kill the farmers' animals. Farmers probably killed them with poisoned arrows or traps.

> **How do we know?**
> Pictures on pottery tablets and seals show that the people of the Indus Valley farmed and raised animals. We learn about the kind of crops the Indus people grew by studying burned grain and by studying the crops planted today in the same areas.

The most dangerous animals around Harappan cities were tigers and leopards. This **tablet** shows a tiger that has chased a man up a tree.

A City in the Indus Valley

Cities in the Indus Valley could be recognized by their massive walls and gateways. Each city was made up of walled sections. The sections contained large public buildings, market areas, homes, and craft workshops. Each major city, or mound, was surrounded by a massive mud-brick wall and brick gateway.

Cities were laid out with straight streets and drains that were supposed to be cleaned regularly. But sometimes they were not cleaned. As streets and drains became clogged and caused water to run into the houses, the lower room of a house was filled with dirt. Another room was then added on top. This is how the mounds built up over hundreds of years.

The city walls were not just for keeping people out. It is likely they were built to keep the town from being flooded during heavy rains. It is also

As houses were added on to and rebuilt, the level of the streets became higher. After many years, the present city was much higher than the original city.

Each city had a drainage system. **Corbeled** arches like this one were built to carry drainage under the streets and buildings to the edge of the city.

thought that walls were built to control **trade.** Different groups of **artisans** or **merchants** often lived in separate, walled sections of the city.

Harappa

Outside the city wall and gateway of Harappa was a small mound containing houses, drains, bathing platforms, and possibly a well. This might have been a rest stop for travelers. The different mounds at Harappa were not all built at the same time, but the people who lived there shared the same **culture.**

Special areas of each city had shops, merchants' houses, and artisans' workshops on streets running north to south. Streets also were oriented east to west. Smaller alleyways led to more private, residential areas.

Bricks

Most buildings in the large cities of the Indus Valley were made of baked brick. There were two sizes of bricks. Small bricks measured 3 x 5.5 x 11 inches (7 x 14 x 28 centimeters). The small bricks were used to build houses. Large bricks were 4 x 8 x 15.5 inches (10 x 20 x 40 centimeters). The large bricks were used to build walls around the settlements and large platforms to raise houses high above the plains. The houses were laid out along wide, straight streets. Some cities, such as Dholavira, used stone instead of bricks.

The Great Bath

One of the outstanding structures of the Indus Valley civilization is the Great Bath at Mohenjo-daro. It was 39 feet (12 meters) long, 23 feet (7 meters) wide, and 8 feet (2.4 meters) deep with steps at two ends. All the bricks of this large tank were carefully ground and fitted together to make a water-tight pool. An extra lining of bitumen (tar) was laid under the bricks to make it even more water tight. The Great Bath was made entirely of brick, except for the doors and windows. They were probably made of wood.

Brick makers

Bricks were probably made by a special group of craftworkers and their families. Children may have helped in brick making. Some bricks have small footprints from children walking on top of the wet clay bricks. Brick maker traditions appear to have extended to other areas. They developed techniques for laying bricks. They also developed uniform brick sizes to build walls with strong bonding and corners.

These brick fragments have children's footprints on them, showing that they may have helped their parents make bricks.

Besides houses, brick makers worked on wells, city walls, gateways, and public buildings. Like most crafts during this time, children were trained to be brick makers by their parents.

Tools

The Harappans had different tools, depending on what material they were working on. For wood, they used copper and bronze axes, chisels, drills, and saws. Tools made out of stone were used for drilling, scraping, and finishing. Harappans used hammers and chisels to shape large stone disks and square stone blocks.

One example of a brick was **inscribed** with a tiger-like design. Bricks with such designs may have been used in special rituals to protect the building.

A typical house

The Harappans liked privacy. A typical house was built with rooms arranged around a central courtyard. Most doorways and windows faced the courtyard. Houses were built so the first story wall along the main street had no windows. Anyone walking on the street could not see into the house, but people on the second floor could look down on the street.

The most common building materials in the Indus Valley were mud brick, baked brick, or stone. Most houses were made of mud brick. Doors were likely made of carved or painted wood. Windows were probably covered with wooden shutters or grillwork. These coverings gave privacy, but let in the light and air.

The floor was usually hard packed dirt that was covered with clean sand or plastered, but some houses had brick floors. Stairs led from the courtyard to the roof or second story. Many houses had two stories. The roof was probably made of wooden beams and covered with reeds and clay. Large houses often had smaller houses around them. These may have been homes for family members or servants.

Archaeologists excavated these brick rooms of a typical Harappan house.

This is an alley in Mohenjo-daro. The individual house drains connect to the main city drain, where sewage flowed out of the city.

Cleanliness

Harappans wanted things clean. On the street side of a house, they built a place to put trash. This was probably collected by street sweepers and carried away to be dumped outside the city walls. Bathing platforms and toilets were connected to drains that led to the main city drains.

Kitchens

There were indoor and outdoor kitchens that would have been used at different times of the year. Indoor kitchens were mainly used for food preparation in the winter. Outdoor kitchens were probably used for preparing larger amounts of food in the summer. Having the oven outside was a way to keep houses cool.

pot for holding water

oval hearth

This kitchen was excavated in the city of Harappa. It has three hearths and a water pot.

round hearth   *square hearth*

Other Cities in the Indus Valley

There were several cities along the Indus River and its **tributaries.** The small town of Lothal, off the coast of west India, had a water **reservoir**. Next to the reservoir was a large house that may have been a warehouse. Lothal was close to the sea and may have been a **trading** center. Ships may have docked in the nearby bay to drop off goods that were then brought upriver to Lothal.

Mohenjo-daro was one of the largest cities in the Indus Valley and was also an important commercial center. Trade and craft making took place there. People from all over the region came to Mohenjo-daro to buy and sell goods.

This water reservoir at Lothal is 700 feet (213 meters) long. It might have played a part in the trade that took place there.

Harappa was another major city with markets and craft workshops. The people

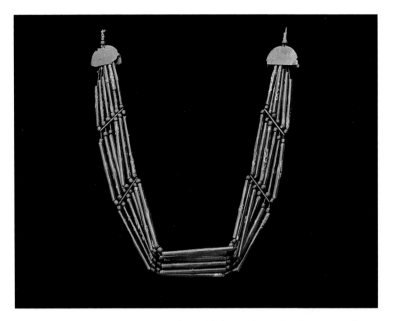

Carnelian is a hard stone. It would take a Harappan over a year to complete a belt of carnelian beads such as this.

who lived there made all kinds of objects for use by local communities and for trade. It was also a meeting place for **merchants** and farmers who came to the city to trade their goods.

Bead makers in the city of Chanhudaro made long beads of **carnelian.** They used a special chipping technique and a very hard, tiny stone drill. Dholavira was another city famous for its beads. It was located on Kadir Island, where it controlled the sea trade to the Indus Valley.

All of these cities were located either along or near rivers. These cities were also important commercial centers. Being near rivers made it easy for merchants to move products from place to place. Many craftworkers, merchants, and traders lived in the major cities.

Cooking and Eating

Food

Harappans ate meat, vegetables, and such grains as barley and wheat. People in some regions may have also eaten rice and **millet**. Animal bones **excavated** in city streets and garbage dumps tell us that people also ate cattle, sheep, goats, and some pigs. **Archaeologists** have found pots that still contain kernels of grain. Food was kept in large storage jars or clay plastered bins. These were usually plain, without painted designs.

Harappans cooked their meals in pots like this.

Cooking

The women and daughters of the house cooked the food both inside and outside the home. In order to keep the house cool, they only cooked small meals inside. They cooked outside when they had to prepare a large amount of food. Men also helped to butcher large animals and prepare food.

The cooking pot this woman is using is very similar to the pots ancient Harappans used.

Eating

Most of the cooking utensils and dishes used by Harappans were made of pottery. Wealthier people used bronze plates. Bronze was more expensive than pottery, but it lasted longer. Sometimes disposable pointed base goblets were used. Harappans probably used knives to cut their food. Since no spoons or forks have been found, we can assume they ate primarily with their hands, as is common in Pakistan and India even today.

Most Harappans had bowls and plates made of terra-cotta. A typical Harappan kitchen might have contained any or all of these items. The perforated container at the back left was a bird cage.

Music

Some musical instruments have been found, as well as some terra-cotta puppets. Instruments that may have been used by the Harappans were conch shell trumpets, terra-cotta whistles, and painted rattles.

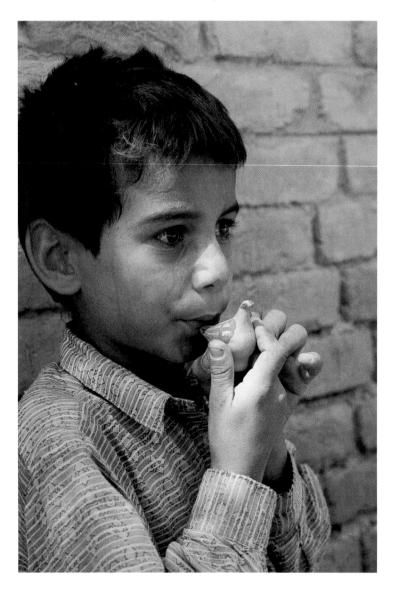

This hollow whistle was made in the form of a bird. It was used for making music and as a child's toy. It might have represented a pet bird.

Dog and bear figurines with protective collars suggest the possibility of animal fights as entertainment.

Games

Various games may have been played in the Indus Valley. Some games that **archaeologists** believe the Harappans played are board games of capture and encirclement, marbles, tops, and dice.

Archaeologists have also found **figurines** of monkeys, dogs, and bears. Toy oxcarts, pulled by movable oxen, resemble the oxcarts still used for transportation and racing in modern Mohenjo-daro.

Traveling performers

Masks and puppets have been found at both Mohenjo-daro and Harappa. These **artifacts** suggest that traveling performers went from city to city, entertaining people. Archaeologists think they dressed in special clothes for their performances.

Pottery

The Harappans were skilled craftworkers. They used a potter's wheel to make pottery. The design of the potter's wheel has not changed in thousands of years.

Pottery was made in every village. It was needed for preparing and storing food. Some pottery was baked and painted with designs and figures. The most common pottery colors were red with black designs. Most pottery was carefully made and fired in specially controlled kilns using wood fires.

This large pot was found in a Harappan burial. The painted design is of trees and other geometric forms.

Copper and bronze

Other craftworkers worked with copper and bronze. Cooking utensils, plates, and **figurines** were sometimes made of bronze. Bronze and copper were used in making spear points and knives.

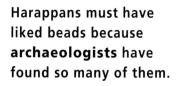

Harappans must have liked beads because **archaeologists** have found so many of them.

Weaving

Cloth was made out of cotton or wool. It was either bleached white or colored with dyes made from plants grown nearby. Cloth impressions left on metal and other objects show the types of weave. Some figurines have painted designs that indicate fabric and color.

Baskets were made from reeds and grasses. **Hemp** fibers were twisted together to make cord. Cords were used to tie bundles and to support pottery as it dried.

Looms

Normal weave is an interlacing of single threads, one thread over, then under the next. This kind of weaving may have been done on a simple loom with bone tools. Hand-turned spinning wheels and traditional looms used today are very much like those used centuries ago in the Indus Valley.

This is an impression of fabric left on a toy bed. The fabric is tightly woven of uniformly spun threads in a normal weave.

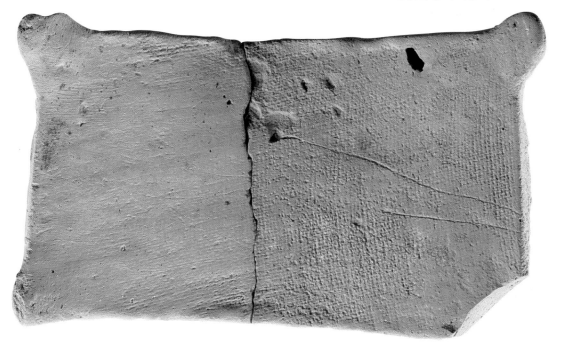

Merchants and traders

Grain, goods, and pottery were **traded** along the Indus River. **Merchants** traded and sold goods. They also collected taxes. Traders carried raw materials into cities and carried finished products out. Traders traveled to faraway places to bring back raw materials such as semi-precious stones and metal ore. Both merchants and traders may have started out as **apprentices.**

Merchants used a standard system of weights and measures. Their system of standardized stone weights was used for business and taxes. This same system of weights is still in use in some traditional markets of Pakistan and India.

This set of cubical weights was carefully made. The Harappans used a standard **binary** weight system in all their transactions.

A Harappan market might have looked like this. These traders are dealing with lapis lazuli and turquoise. The merchant is weighing beads.

Barter

Artisans made objects with the raw materials traders brought into the cities from distant lands. They then traded the objects they made for grain and food. The Harappans did not use money. They used a system of barter—trading a service for another service or food. Stones such as agate and **carnelian** were used in trade. They were also used as items for barter. Other rare materials, such as **lapis lazuli** and **turquoise,** were also used for barter.

Roads

Nearly every city in the Indus Valley was laid out with wide, straight streets. The side lanes were narrow but straight. Once outside the city, a traveler had to walk for about one day before reaching the next town. If he wanted to go to the nearest big city, it would usually take several days or even weeks to get there.

This is one of the narrow side streets that was **excavated** at Mohenjo-daro.

No one knows whether the roads were made of anything besides dirt. **Archaeologists** have found ancient cart tracks on some streets. If a road was traveled often, the dirt would be packed hard most of the time. In the rain, the roads were almost impossible to travel. The roads became slippery and carts could not be pulled through the thick mud. After the rain stopped, the roads dried quickly. Ruts left from cart wheels made walking on the roads difficult.

Caravans

Caravans of pack animals brought supplies and goods to the cities. At Harappa, there was a small settlement outside one of the ancient gateways. It is possible that this settlement was a rest stop for caravans. The modern road running along the southern edge of Harappa was first used by caravans more than 4,500 years ago.

Bridges

Harappans did not build bridges across large rivers. If they needed to cross the river, they used boats. Some of the flat-bottomed riverboats used oars and sails. Along the coast, the ships used different sails.

The countryside outside modern Harappa looks much the same as it did during ancient Harappan times.

Elephants may have been occassionally used for travel. Usually, farmers carried their products to market in a cart pulled by two **bullocks.** The same type of cart was often used to carry a bride to her new home. This type of cart is still being used today.

Boats

Flat-bottomed boats were used on the river to carry goods to the coast. When going upriver, bullocks may have pulled the boats from the bank. Some boats may have had long oars and sails of heavy cotton. Some **seals** show boats with separate cabins and a ladder to the roof. A high seated platform at the stern made it possible for someone to move the rudder.

Wheeled carts were used to transport goods and people in rural areas. Miniature carts like this one were used by children as toys. These toys tell us how the Harappans traveled and transported goods.

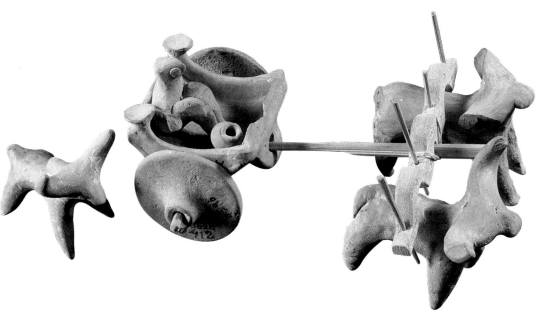

Carrying goods

Caravans of pack animals carried goods from the mountains of the west to the Indus Valley. On the plains, carts pulled by **zebu** carried heavy goods to the cities from the farms and small towns. Men and women also hauled **trade** goods to market. They would walk to the market with their goods and return home with grain and other items.

Carts

Ancient oxcarts were made of wood with rawhide and leather bindings for a harness. Axles and solid wheels were joined together, rotating as a single unit. This type of traditional oxcart is still in use today.

These men are transporting goods with a cart similar to those used by the ancient Harappans.

Trade and Trade Routes

The cities along the Indus River had towers that rose above the city walls. Watchmen in the towers could see travelers as they came to the city.

Traders

Traders coming overland usually traveled in **caravans.** Their goods were packed onto the backs of cattle, sheep, or goats. Some brought their grain or goods in carts pulled by **bullocks.**

Most of the Indus Valley trade supplied the cities with food and necessary raw materials for making tools, **figurines,** and trade goods. Many of the raw materials were obtained from nearby regions.

Harappans traded extensively throughout the Indus Valley. They also traded outside of the area. All of the major cities were along trade routes.

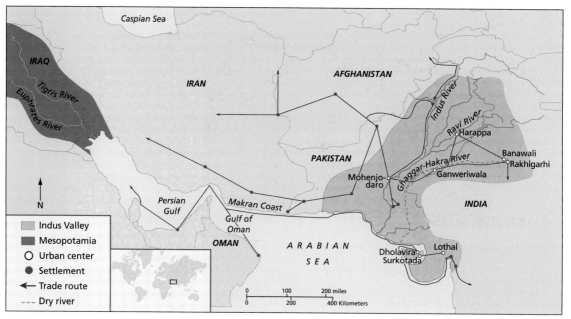

The people of Harappa traded with people near **chert** quarries in the central Indus Valley. They traded with shell collectors of the **Makran** coast, too. Copper was mined in the western mountains or even as far as Oman.

Trade routes

Some Harappan traders traveled across the sea to Oman and up the Persian Gulf to Mesopotamia. There was some limited overland trade through southern Iran. Indus Valley **artifacts** have been found in Oman and along the southern coast of the Arabian Gulf. **Seals** from the Arabian Gulf region have been found in the Indus Valley. This shows that there was trade between the regions.

This is the coastline of Makran, along the Arabian Sea. Harappans traded from this area to Oman for only a short period of time.

Major trade goods from Oman were copper, shell, dates, incense, and possibly mother-of-pearl. The Harappans probably sent grains, livestock, butter, honey, and fresh fruit in return. This trade with Oman became very important between 2200 and 2100 B.C.E.

The Harappans may have received wool, incense, and gold from Mesopotamia. In return, they sent **carnelian** beads, shell **bangles,** ivory, and **lapis lazuli.**

Weapons

The people of the Indus Valley did not have large armies. The weapons they did have were probably mostly used for hunting. Most weapons were copper spears and knives, bone arrow points, and stone **mace** heads.

It is possible that local arguments resulted in the raiding of other villages, but there have been no paintings or other evidence found showing battles. **Archaeologists** have not found any record of taking captives either.

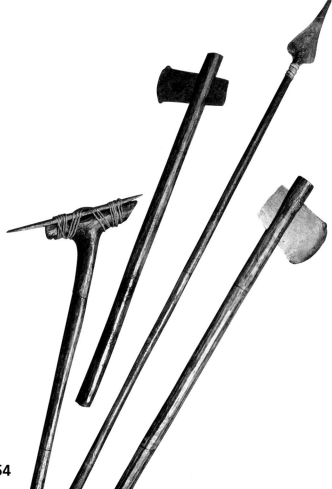

These copper and bronze weapons and tools were found at Harappa. The wooden handles are modern additions to show how they would have looked.

City walls

Harappans managed well in the cities. Even though they had walls around the city, there is nothing to show that the walls were built for defense. The walls were most likely built for protection against floods and also to control the traffic into the city. There were many gateways to control movement into and out of the cities.

Some **sites** show layers of ash that indicate a big fire. These sites have been rebuilt during ancient times. The ash does not seem to be a result of war, but more likely accidental causes.

These archaeologists are **excavating** city walls in Harappa. They believe that the walls were not meant as protection from enemies, but rather for control of **trade.**

The Best of Times

The years from 2600 to 1900 B.C.E. are the high point of the Indus Valley civilization. The ancient cities **excavated** from that time were large. The cities are found scattered over an area twice the size of ancient Egypt or Mesopotamia. During these years, the Indus Valley cities and their settlements dominated the region of what is now Pakistan and northern India.

The neighbors of the Indus Valley cities were fighting wars and building great palaces and temples. There is no archaeological evidence that the people of the Indus Valley did this. They built their cities and made laws. They developed ways of distributing food and

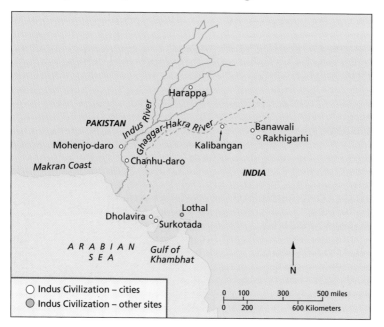

The major **sites** of the Indus Valley are shown on this map.

water to the people. They even had a way of disposing of waste and garbage. The Harappan communities grew from a farming tradition and became wealthy through **trade.** Harappans learned to solve problems. They educated their children, took care of extra food, and were a relatively peaceful people.

The Harappans did not have a central temple or palace. There are no written texts or elaborate burial ceremonies. They did not bury valuable objects with the dead, preferring to keep them in use with the living. What sets the Harappans apart from other civilizations is the absence of warfare and taking of captives.

Harappa was a large, thriving city for several hundred years. This illustration shows what the city might have looked like.

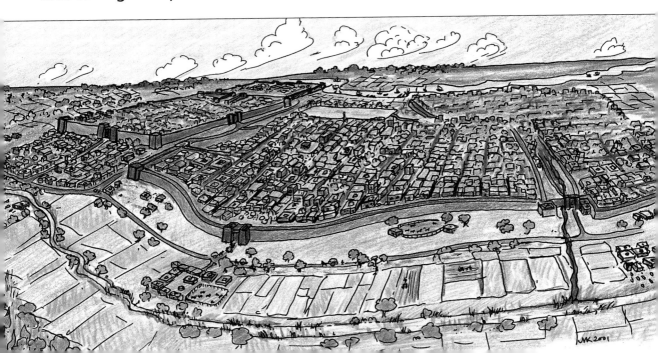

Weather

The Harappan civilization might have declined due to changes in weather and geography. It is possible that an earthquake caused the Indus and Ghaggar-Hakra Rivers to change direction. When new riverbeds are formed, there are large floods. The pattern of rainfall might have changed. Grain would not have been able to grow in the changed land.

Lack of trade

A weakening of the agricultural base for the cities might have contributed to the breakdown of **trade.** Wealth no longer came into the country because of this lack of trade. Some people began to leave the region and move east and south.

Trade also could have broken down because the river's new direction changed the shipping routes. **Artifacts** such as **inscribed seals,** weights, and pointed base goblets stopped appearing in markets. Some Harappans still made shell **bangles,** beads, and ornaments, but none of these were traded over great distances like before.

This flooding of the Indus River near Mohenjo-daro is the result of the river changing its course.

There is general agreement on what caused the Harappan civilization to decline and eventually disappear. It is likely that some natural forces weakened the society, and later human actions aided in the decline.

Legacy of the Indus Valley

The Indus Valley civilization has disappeared, but its legacy remains. Many of the traditional arts and crafts methods can be seen in the works of present-day India and Pakistan. Wearing bangles and beads and using conch shell trumpets are still common.

This man is playing a conch shell trumpet, just as the Harappans probably did long ago.

There is evidence of the ancient Indus Valley **culture** in the tile work and weaving of India and Pakistan. Even though the Harappan civilization is gone, it lives on in various ways throughout the Indus River region.

This method of tile work has survived for centuries, adapted to the materials of the Indus Valley.

B.C.E.

7000   Settlements began to appear in the Indus Valley region. People began to **cultivate** wheat, barley, and other crops. They also began to raise cattle, sheep, and goats.

5500–2800   Settlements spread more widely in the Indus Valley. The following crafts emerged during this period: metalworking, ceramics, **lapidary** arts, glazed **faience, seal** making and the development of hand-built and wheel-thrown pottery.
Trade networks established with neighboring regions. People buried with tools and animals.

2800–2600   First city seen at Harappa.

2600–2500   Earliest trade contacts with Ur in southern Mesopotamia.

2600–1900   Height of the Harappan civilization and emergence of Indus cities: Mohenjo-daro, Harappa, and Dholavira.
Many ceramic **artifacts** and jewelry from this time period have been found.
Animal **sacrifices** end and **figurines** are buried with the dead instead.
From 2200 to 2100, most trade with Oman took place, as trade with Mesopotamia continued.

1900–1300   The Harappan civilization began to change and new cities emerged.

1300–600   Development of "Vediz" culture and new cities appeared in the Ganges river plain.

Harappan Script

The Harappan **script** remains a mystery to scholars and **archaeologists**. No one has been able to **decipher** the script. Once someone does decipher the script, we will learn a lot more about who the Harappans were and what their **culture** was like. Until that time comes, people will have to rely on other archaeological evidence to learn about the Harappans. Below are just a few of the more than 400 symbols that make up the Harappan script.

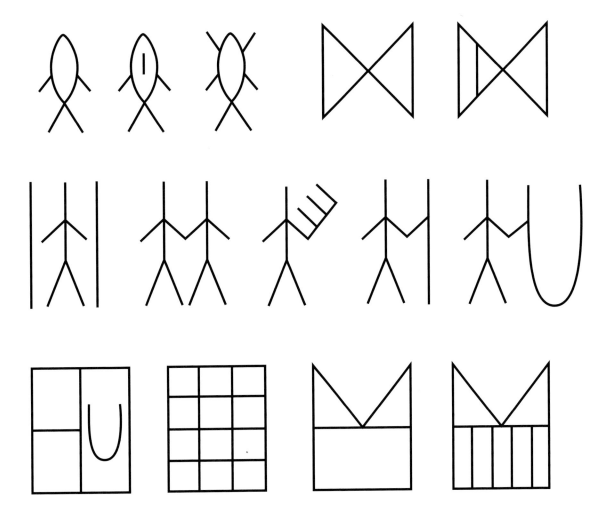

Glossary

apprentice person learning a trade or occupation

archaeologist person who studies the remains of the past such as tools, pottery, and bones

artifact object made by humans

artisan person skilled in arts or craftwork

bangle rigid bracelet or anklet without a clasp

binary something made of or based on two things or parts

bullock young bull

caravan group of people traveling together for safety

carnelian hard, translucent stone that has a reddish color

chert rock containing quartz

corbel bracket of stone, wood, or other building material projecting from a wall. It is used to support a corner or arch.

cultivate to prepare and use soil for growing crops

culture way of life

decipher to figure out the meaning of something

deity god or goddess

excavate to carefully dig up buried objects in order to find out about the past

faience earthenware decorated with colorful glazes, usually greenish-blue

fertility ability to have children

figurine small statue

hemp type of plant with stem fibers that can be woven into cloth

incantation charm or spell recited to produce a magic effect

inscribe to cut letters, numbers, or patterns into a solid surface

irrigation watering of crops by channeling water from a river or lake along pipes and ditches

lapidary person who cuts, polishes, or engraves gems

lapis lazuli semi-precious stone of deep blue

mace heavy war club with a spiked head

Makran dry, rugged coastal region of Pakistan and Iran

merchant person who buys and sells goods

millet plant that gives a large crop of grain seeds, used for food

offering something given as a part of worship

Punjab region of northwest India and north Pakistan

reservoir artificial lake

sacrifice to kill an animal or person as an offering to a god or goddess

script system of writing

seal small stone object with pictures or words used to make impressions in tablets

sesamum (also called sesame) tropical Asian plant that bears small flat seeds used as food and to make oil

site area where something was found or took place

tablet flat piece of clay or stone with words or pictures on it

trade to buy and sell goods; person who makes a living by buying and selling goods is a trader

tributary stream that flows into a larger stream or river

turban long scarf wound around the head

turquoise blue to blue-green mineral prized as a gemstone when polished

zebu Asian ox used for work and for milk

More Books to Read

McIntosh, Jane. *Archaeology.* New York: Dorling Kindersley Publishing, 2000.

Nelson, Julie. *India.* Austin, Tex.: Raintree Steck-Vaughn, 2001.

Stewart, Melissa. *Science in Ancient India.* Danbury, Conn.: Franklin Watts, 1999.

Index